LEAD YOU

NOTES TO YOUNG AFRICANS ON CREATING A MORE REPRESENTATIVE CONTINENT

UFUOMA OTU

Acknowledgements

The more important a call to action is to our soul's evolution, the more resistance we will feel about answering it. But to yield to Resistance deforms our spirit. It stunts us and makes us less than we are and were born to be.

Steven Pressfield

I felt the gravity of that quote in the writing of *Lead You*. There were lots of starts and stops, but thankfully I felt called to stick to it because of the direct and indirect influence of the following:

Infinite God, the source of all life, the purest inspirations, machinations, and mercy; there are no words to fully express my utmost gratitude.

My family, who taught and reinforced to me that leadership always starts from going within, I am tremendously grateful.

Augustine Blay, who, when I shared the inspiration for this book, mirrored back to me that such a book is needed. I picked up the ball and embarrassingly dropped it, but our pivotal conversation about the subject matter made sure that I would successfully pick it up again.

Beloved Publishing House, no sooner had I put out the intent for an editor that was culturally aware and sensitive to the subject matter did I serendipitously stumble into your past work. Thank you for delivering so precisely.

The wonderful staff at Vestar Coffee and My Coffee House in Lagos, I appreciate you for consistently providing a safe and comfortable space for the second half of *Lead You* to materialize.

The young African leaders continuing to forge forward despite all odds and the ones wonderfully growing in consciousness, I hope *Lead You* helps hold space for you. Know it's 110% yours!!

Contents

"It's time Africa started listening to our young people instead of always telling them what to do."

Mo Ibrahim

A Note to the Reader

Once marred with disease and poverty, the African continent is gradually transforming into one of hope and opportunity. Any major international business publication will tell you

Figure 1: Partial View of Africa on Globe.
James Wiseman/Unsplash

this: things are happening on the continent. Industries are experiencing impressive growth. The demographic of many African countries is young, dynamic, and pulsating with energy. They are infusing various industries, from entertainment, and telecommunications to fashion and finance, with vigor. Against this momentum hangs a political landscape that has proven unable to keep up.

After several decades of so-called independence from

colonial rule, representative government has largely remained elusive, mocked, and compromised by systemic corruption and political tyranny. Slowly, widespread apathy resulting from years of living under these harsh realities is giving way to Africans, particularly younger Africans, who, emboldened by technological advances in media, especially social media, are speaking out against deplorable leadership and governance that ignore their needs and actively rob them of a brighter future.

Indeed, the future ought to be brighter for a continent that consistently ranks as having the youngest demographic in the world. According to the African Union, more than 400 million people on the continent are between the ages of 15 and 35[i]. In comparison, the average age of African leaders is around 62 years. Hardly a negative but problematic because it's the norm and the vast disconnect between older (mis)leaders[*1] who preserve a status quo that inherently benefits their cohorts rather than adapt and implement policies that include and reflect the socio-economic advancement of their younger populace. Therein lies one of

---

[1] * The (mis)leader spelling is intentional and meant to call attention to the practice of liberally calling them "leaders" plays a role in normalizing their bad leadership.

the most significant challenges the African continent has encountered in the 21st century. Increasingly more educated, technologically savvy, and more interconnected with the rest of the world than previous generations, Africa's young adults are impatient with business as usual. Now they have more tools at their disposal to express discontent that is readily captured on the global stage, to the chagrin of their governments. Like their Arab Spring cohorts a decade ago, young leaders were at the core of the #EndSARs movement against Nigerian government-sanctioned police brutality, widespread support in Uganda for Bobi Wine's unprecedented challenge of Yoweri Museveni's 35-year rule, Diane Rigwara audaciously challenged Paul Kagame's governance in Rwanda and Nelson Chamisa of Emmerson Mnangagwa's in Zimbabwe[ii].

More African leaders of tomorrow are pushing to take their seats at the proverbial table and advocating for their interests. However, how they accomplish this feat is based on the future they would like to create. And how effectively we create this future will be based on the mindsets we adopt now and the tools with which we take ownership.

The African continent has a well-documented track record of what hasn't worked. Greed and corruption have essentially undermined the wealthiest continent in the world in terms of natural resources. Holding fast to outdated tribal, ethnic, and religious divisions continues to set African countries back in ways many Africans still can't even comprehend. That lack of understanding extends to Africans' understanding of the complex outcomes of the continent's colonial past.

A way forward is developing a firmer grasp of that not-too-distant past and realizing while colonialism and political (mis)leadership get the lion's share of the blame for the continent's present-day ills, being adept at apportioning blame without attempting to tackle these ills with courageous commitment is a colossal waste of time at best and self-esteem annihilation at worst.

Ultimately, a successful Africa is one that maximizes the talents and contributions of all its citizenry – young and old(er). Such leadership and governance ought to be representative of the governed for an Africa that, in the words of Nelson Mandela, is "in peace with itself."[iii]

It will take tremendous responsibility and vision – a crucial characteristics of the great African leaders of today and tomorrow. This book is written for their encouragement, success, and the realization that nothing will change unless we do. Thank you for having and keeping an open mind as you read it.

"If a leader loves you, he makes sure you build your house on a rock."

Ugandan Proverb

Chapter 1:

Leadership Is Not Out There—It's in You

When you think of a leader – a good leader – who comes to mind? If you are like many people, someone else probably came to mind. Someone whom you deeply admire. A colleague, celebrity, loved one or friend, or even a boss or supervisor at work. And they probably came to mind because of a distinct trait – tangible or intangible. They are charismatic and personable. Maybe they are visionaries in their thought process. Or they are dedicated, hardworking, selfless, and kind. The list goes on. Generally, when we think of good leaders, we think of people we consider the salt of the earth. They are seemingly perfect in many ways. Even though we are aware that no human being is perfect, there's this need to put good leaders on a pedestal because we all fall short in some way. Or perhaps only then would they be truly worthy of our admiration or praise. The truth is everyone, including you, is capable of being a good leader. Of course, it requires conscious effort and lifelong commitment. Sometimes you won't feel like much of a leader at all. But no need to get too far ahead of ourselves. For starters, who is a leader, and why would you want to become one?

Simply put, a leader is one who guides and shows the way – directly or indirectly. One doesn't have to have a ton of followers to lead and do so effectively.

Figure 2: Young African Colleagues. Pixabay

You can lead your life according to specific principles and values. Your approach to leadership can extend to your family life, workplace, and immediate community of friends, neighbors, etc. When you lead your life and actions in such a way that it has a positive effect on those around you, you are already on your way to being a leader. As a leader, you are always improving, learning, and growing. This continuous improvement not only improves your life but those around you because you become an example of how to be. By example, you inspire others - your peers, younger people, and even those older than you. It causes a ripple effect you may not always be aware of, but one that happens, nonetheless.

A leader holds themselves to high standards of conduct. Of the many qualities attributed to effective leaders, self-awareness and character are at the top of the list. Effective leaders are self-aware. They know their strengths and areas of improvement, which means they don't condemn themselves but are clear about the areas where they need help; their self-awareness facilitates their ability to connect with and inspire others. As for the second quality, the essence of any individual is their character. Leadership expert John C. Maxwell refers to "character" as a choice: "Character is more than talk. Anyone can say that he has integrity, but action is the real indicator of character. Your character determines who you are. That's why you can never separate a leader's character from his actions. If a leader's actions and intentions are continuously working against each other, then look to [their] character to find out why."[iv]

How do you act when no one's watching? Do you challenge yourself to do the right thing often? When you look around your community, do you only see opportunities to complain, or do you challenge yourself to look for solutions to various big and small problems? A good leader is action-oriented; they are more than willing to roll up their sleeves and take any initiative to which they are committed to new heights.

You can also start separating yourself from the notion that leadership is only found in other people. Or that it only matters on grandiose scales. Leadership is a mindset everyone – young and mature – can adopt. It's great to have mentors, people you admire and who inspire you to do and be more. But whether they are readily available or afar, never lose touch with your own inner fortitude. The same qualities you are seeking in other leaders, you can cultivate within. The same actions you want other leaders to take, you can initiate in your own way. Leadership can become a way of life, and why not? Every leader begins with leading their own life. They have a vision for their lives and how it fits into the larger society and vice versa.

What's in Your Leadership Toolkit?

Leadership in the African continent in past years, especially in the political arena, has been tied to a select few. In the past decade, technology and industry have created opportunities for leaders from all walks of life to be recognized, ushering broader perspectives of what it entails to be a leader. In yesteryears, leadership was inextricably tied to authority - over information and resources - but the tide is shifting. Where outcry and demand for accountability had largely fallen on deaf ears in the past, social media channels make it virtually impossible for criticism from the masses to be completely swept under the rug as in previous decades. With these tools come responsibility: on the one hand, they can be used to assess the track record of (mis)leaders almost in real-time, but they also provide opportunities to assess how the populace contributes to the environment it says it desires.

We can take advantage of opportunities to lead, and there are many. How and if we recognize them depends on us.

Figure 3: A young African woman. iStock

Explore your background and experiences. What unique

perspectives can you bring to the table as a leader? You have spheres of influence. How have you tapped into or galvanized them?

Admittedly an oversimplification, subscription to the Machiavellian leadership philosophy of the "end justifies the means," has wreaked horrors in the continent, but other seemingly less avowed aspects of his insight still hold true.

"There are classes of intellect: one which comprehends itself; another which appreciates what others comprehend; and a third which neither comprehends by itself nor by the show of others; the first is excellent, the second is good, and the third is useless."[v]

What category describes you? Hopefully, it's the first or second, or a mix of both. But not the third. Young African leaders experience life aware of the challenges that prevail but are also learning about and creating opportunities that abound within the challenges. Often uncovered in the aftermath of frustration or in a moment of inspired creativity, young people increasingly have the flexibility and technical know-how and are steadily growing the courage to embrace the opportunities.

If we can lead, how should we do it? Well, in all the ways

that maximize our abilities and advance our society. Since leadership is more than a title, it's what we do with it that counts. One can hardly call themselves a leader if nothing in their environment changes: the past and current crop of African (mis)leaders have shown us that.

A good leader observes their environment to decipher what type of leadership style would be advantageous. Are you willing to be adaptable and engage in the dance of adopting leadership styles that could work in one situation and another that would be more effective in a different scenario?

Be clear on what your fundamental principles and values are but be flexible. Young African leaders are in a unique position to fuse the best of core cultural-based leadership traits –responsibility for yourself, family, uprightness, and not bringing shame to the family handed down from our families and communities – with individual self-actualization.

How you express this fusion depends on the variety of factors that affect your life. There is no one right way; rather, adapt to each situation, especially since you will likely be working with others with different skill sets and leadership styles. Focus on the "what" of the issue to be addressed and then the "how". Think of specific actions alongside their consequences. Strive to make the best decisions after considering all the information and facts you have at your disposal. Commitment to your vision and a roll-up-your-sleeve attitude can help you go the distance.

What existing resources can you tap into? For example, explore initiatives that interweave development and diaspora; entrepreneurship and investment, philanthropy; innovation; or volunteerism. Are there organizations that connect talented youth in your community with the African diaspora providing constituents with special invitations, professional development workshops, networking opportunities, job announcements, and access to influential voices?

If not, would you consider starting or combining efforts with others to jumpstart one? What about offering leadership, personal development, and mentoring resources to African students to foster the next generation of African leaders?

By analyzing government policy initiatives, exploring knowledge transfer opportunities, and mobilizing public and private sector groups, youth-founded organizations can inform and educate the public about the effect of local policies on constituents. Such organizations can eventually drive the necessary grassroots mobilization that can spur the passage of legislation that affect millions of African lives.

Access to mobile technology and social media has transformed how people consume information and exchange ideas. Utilizing social media as a vehicle of advocacy and change has become the norm. With creativity, ingenuity, passion, and persistence, young people are starting cause campaigns on social media every day. More than 130 million people use Facebook each month in the African continent – with 98% accessing it through their mobile phones.[vi] In 2022, more than 218 million were active on YouTube[vii] and 22 million on Twitter[viii].

As a result, to help correct the misinformation and misconception of the African continent, a young Ghanaian woman took to Twitter with #TheAfricaTheMediaNeverShowsYou several years ago.[ix] The hashtag caught on and was featured on many international news sources as part of the ongoing discourse on why the all-doom and negative media coverage of the continent needs to be updated and balanced with an emphasis on the positive characteristics and developments the African continent also boasts. With the #TheAfricaTheMediaNeverShowsYou, these young people simply and creatively captured in assorted photos the vibrancy of different aspects of their continent, highlighting everything from stunning natural beauty to diversity in socio-economic investment opportunities.

#TheAfricaTheMediaNeverShowsYou several years ago is one campaign, but there are opportunities for many more. The continent needs new stereotypes – positive stereotypes. As the maxim goes, if you say something often enough, it becomes the truth. That is partially the case with the enduring narrative about the continent. However, it can be aided by a young generation of African leaders embracing their role in rebranding the continent.

What kinds of positive stereotypes do you want to represent or help create?

There is a plethora of best practices to glean from to effectively leverage social media tools for such initiatives. Take advantage of social tools with an eye toward how they can help advance the core objectives of the initiatives you care most about to ensure strong stakeholder engagement and connectivity. Remember, social media channels are important avenues to not just criticize current (mis)leaders but support innovative leadership campaigns and raise awareness about them.

Rwanda is a country that has rolled up its sleeves and taken on the intensive process of rebranding its image. The country's well-known civil war escalated and resulted in the genocidal mass slaughter of between 500,000 to 1 million Tutsis by a Hutu majority government in 1994. How does a country recover from such atrocity?

Led by Paul Kagame – whose increasingly autocratic regime and ambitions for a fourth term[x] in office have earned him a growing number of critics – Rwanda emerged as one of the least

Figure 4: Paul Kagame speaks at a youth entrepreneurship townhall meeting in 2019. KT Press

corrupt governments in Africa, according to Transparency International[xi]. Rwanda also has more women leaders in government than any other country in the world[xii]. It revamped its educational system to provide universal education to children, including children orphaned by the genocide and more. Speaking of positive stereotypes, Rwanda has picked up some too. International visitors to the country marvel at its orderliness and cleanliness[xiii].

When asked about his philosophical approach to rebuilding Rwanda post-genocide, Kagame admits he doesn't have it all figured out. "There is no strategy manual for this. There is nothing that is not a priority, and the priorities are always conflicting. I try to look at problems very clearly and think, 'How do we get out of this? What will work? What will be the consequences for the people involved[xiv]?'"

One would be hard-pressed to find any leader who is perfect. Kagame certainly isn't, not with the growing concerns about his "uncompromising approach to democracy"[xv].

Hard as it can be at times, we don't always have to agree 100 percent with others' approaches or perspectives to be able to collaborate with them, nor do we negate all the positive aspects and outcomes of their leadership approach by focusing solely on what we don't agree with. There's no doubt Kagame's strong, forward-focused vision for Rwanda has helped the country get back on its feet.

"You will always hear me talking about the importance of dignity," Kagame said. "It is really the key to people's lives." [xvi] And he is right about that because with dignity comes a sense of ownership.

This dignity should inform our self-perception beyond lip service - it should reflect in how we lead and how we perceive each other (more to come on that).

Not taking anything away from the African ambassadors who have served and continue to serve around the world, but we are all cultural ambassadors directly or indirectly representing our countries of origin. To the extent that we can consistently do so in positive ways, we deploy soft power. This shouldn't be underestimated; in many ways, it is an extraordinary influence if utilized wisely.

The African continent and diaspora are teeming with young people – there is significant strength in these numbers – who are already making an impact and can continue to do so in even greater capacities. Remember, no matter how long you live; you will never know it all. Let that be your challenge to keep learning and growing. Learn from your experiences, learn from the mistakes of others, and learn from your peers and good forebears. Focus on your commonality with other young leaders instead of your differences. And as resident trendsetters, embrace your role in the one area the African continent sorely needs and still lacks – veritable leadership.

"Only a wise person can solve a difficult problem."

Akan Proverb

Chapter 2:

West, East, North & South – Where We Are Today

If the continent of Africa were an airplane, it was supposed to take off in 1960. This was the year that was dubbed the 'Year of Africa.'

Figure 5: Partial Map of African continent

Seventeen African nations gained their independence that year. What must it have felt like walking in the streets, experiencing the jubilation, the air pregnant with… possibility? In the foreground was a palpable atmosphere of hope and triumph, but in the background was trepidation.

Derailed by corruption, greed, abuse of power, lack of vision, and overall mental malaise, that airplane never really took off. Within less than a decade of independence, many African countries were in jeopardy. It seemed the second 'Scramble for Africa' was taking place, this time not by the colonial powers but by African leaders themselves. Founding nationalist leaders Kwame Nkrumah (Ghana), Gamal Abdel Nasser (Egypt), Leopold Senghor (Senegal), Houphouet-Boigny (Ivory Coast), Felix Sekou Toure (Guinea), Modibo Keita (Mali), Sylvanus Olympio (Togo), Uhuru Kenyatta (Kenya), Julius Nyerere (Tanzania), Kenneth Kaunda (Zambia), Hastings Banda (Malawi) basked in the adoration and great honor that came with the position in the first days after independence but struggled to define ideologies that could maintain let alone transform their countries. Although powerful and ambitious, their administrations morphed into autocratic regimes from seemingly innocuous single-party systems that were supposed to represent unity since African communities were intrinsically communal.

'The Fate of Africa: A History of Fifty Years of Independence,' one of the most seminal historical works on the continent, notes:

In one country after another, African leaders acted in contempt of constitutional rules and agreements they had sworn to uphold to enhance their own power. Constitutions were either amended or rewritten, or simply ignored. Checks and balances were removed. Nkrumah's first amendment to the constitution – abolishing regional assemblies – was introduced only two years after independence.

In their quest for greater control, the device they commonly favored was the one-party system. In some cases, one-party systems were achieved by the popular verdict. In pre-independence elections in francophone Africa in 1959, Houphouet-Boigny's *Parti Democratique de la Cote d'Ivoire* won all seats in the Legislative assembly; so too did Senghor's *Union Progressiste Senegalaise*, Keita's *Union Soudanaise* in Mali and Bourguiba's *Neo-Destour* in Tunisia. In East Africa, Nyerere's Tanganyika African Union National won all open seats in parliament in 1960; and in the 1964 elections, Banda's Malawi Congress Party also swept the board. In other cases, one-party systems were arranged by negotiation, whereby opposition parties accepted a merger with ruling parties. Sekou Toure's *Parti Democratique de Guinee* won fifty-six in the Legislative Assembly elections in 1957, and the following year, he arranged for opposition politicians to join the PDG. In Kenya in 1964, Kenyatta persuaded opposition politicians from the Kenya African Democratic Union to cross the floor and take up prominent posts in the government. There were many other examples, however, of where one-party systems were imposed simply by suppressing opposition parties – as in Ghana, Niger, Dahomey, Togo, Mauritania, Central African Republic, and Upper Volta (Burkina Faso).[xvii]

A mixture of overreliance on post-colonial economic structures and subsequent mismanagement ensured the decline of an already shaky decolonization process, adding a growing population to the mix, unfavorable trade terms with former colonial powers, and one school of thought would argue that maybe "independence" was premature. Another could argue, what leadership models did the newly minted countries have to go on? For decades they experienced reality as pawns in the colonial quest for the acquisition of agricultural and mineral resources. Colonial imperialism meant whoever was emperor dictated what to do with a specific country's resources. But it happened, and we cannot change the past. However, we can learn from it and strive to grow and move forward. Blaming colonialism for all the ills of African countries can only go so far. Poor leadership and economic mismanagement are largely at the root of Africa's problems – thankfully, we can do something about it.

Today's African leaders, born in that era of hope outlined above, are far removed from the realities and aspirations of the everyday citizen living in their countries. While written constitutions exist, the unwritten versions are even stronger. In the unwritten constitution, the leader is all-powerful, with the position of the presidency wielding absolute power over the people it's supposed to serve. This model of "leadership" drastically needs to change to one where leaders are held accountable to the people they are supposed to lead and serve. While no perfect democratic government exists anywhere in the world, African citizenry should choose – and choose wisely – the African leaders who can fill these shoes. Opt for leaders who are visionaries, competent, possess the courage to say and outline what needs to be done, and can curb their personal greed; leaders who can resist the urge to abuse their power; leaders who believe in their countries and in the African continent. Shun "leaders" who say one thing to get elected and do nothing (or the opposite) of what they promised. Turn away from the so-called leaders that implement a different brand of the same 'divide and conquer' agenda by emphasizing community differences rather than focusing on commonalities.

Fiscally, corruption remains deep-rooted and is the bane of many African countries because it's modeled by leaders and trickles down to everyday life.

In Ghana, for example, ministers pushed contracts with foreign corporations for a 10 percent commission and flaunted their subsequent windfall. In Nigeria, the perception of government as a source of "free money" meant those in political office had access to immense funding that bankrolled party and personal initiatives.[xviii]

In this present day, without functional checks and balances in place, it's almost impossible to weed out corruption. To be clear, there aren't any corruption-free nations in the world; the problem lies in corrupt practices being the norm rather than the exception. Obviously, this won't change quickly, but it can if we all hold ourselves to higher standards of conduct. The average African is seemingly always quick to blame African government leaders for every ill in society, and there is a lot of blame to apportion there. However, governments around the world have not always been the purveyors of change – they have to be compelled by the will and needs of the people to change. For example, the United States government, at a point in time, supported the heinous act of slavery and the Jim Crow laws that were the aftermath of the practice. Neither did the governments in power launch the civil rights movements in the U.S. or in South Africa.

Like in the era of hope, after decades plagued by dictatorships, wide-scale poverty, disease, and fiscal mismanagement, some African countries are experiencing a second renaissance of sorts. African countries are now making the list of the

Figure 6: Brain drain continues to plague the continent. Sustainable Economy

fastest-growing economies released by reputable business and international media outlets. While it might be tempting to take this for granted now, this was hardly the case barely 15 to 20 years ago, where except for South Africa, the rest of the continent, especially sub-Saharan Africa, were sub-par economic entities propped up more or less by foreign aid.

Fortunately, increased awareness of the economic opportunities on the continent enhanced by technology, made accessible by an unprecedented growth of global air travel, and fueled by international free trade agreements have exponentially given Africa a leg up in global competition.

Further, for all the talk about brain drain, there is a growing number of educated and accomplished African immigrants – young and older – returning to their home countries to live and invest. All of this is contributing to an Africa that is growing - even with its current challenges – and has a place on the emerging markets frontier. With this "second renaissance" come opportunities and responsibilities to advocate for sustainable socio-economic changes that benefit all Africans.

As in the era of independence, we cannot afford to squander our opportunities. Young African leaders must resist the temptation to take the path of least resistance by doing only what's expedient politically, socially, and economically. The common saying, 'Rome wasn't built in a day,' has been long used to justify failure and inadequacy. Yes, important initiatives take time. But in addition to time, we need better ideas for the future countries, cities, and localities we would like to create.

"Africa is at once more than a country and less than one…Africa is a concept, pregnant with the dreams of millions of people."

Ali Mazrui

Chapter 3:

How Do We Move Forward?

The two decades following the independence era were punctuated by poignant personalities and events. In Nigeria, the six-month-long Biafra War imperiled the country's fragile republic. Ethiopia's Haile

Figure 7: *Independence Square, Accra, Ghana. George Apphia/Flickr*

Selassie, arguably the most revered African leader of that era and one of its longest-reigning monarchs, died. When the end of his controversial rule came in 1979, Uganda's Idi Amin was perceived as an anti-Western imperialism hero in the continent and a vicious tyrannical leader by the West. In Tanzania, Julius Nyerere experimented with socialism. Back in Ethiopia, Colonel Mengistu Haile Mariam's agricultural products scheme and drought created a perfect storm that ushered in the devastating famine of 1984, in which an estimated one million died. The drought also had disastrous consequences in Sudan, which had already experienced a civil war that resulted in a peace agreement that lasted for eleven years but dissolved into another civil war between the north and south. Sudan's Jaafar Nimeiri, who ignored the aftermath of the drought until mass hunger killed nearly 250,000,[xix] was left with a steep agricultural production deficit and insurmountable debt to foreign countries. In Libya, an army coup launched Muammar Gaddafi into power – he would reign for 42 years.

Although believed to have originated in the Democratic Republic of Congo in the 1920s, AIDS was not fully recognized on the African continent until the 1980s – the full magnitude of the disease would not become apparent until the 1990s, when the death toll numbered in the millions. Before then, the slow-acting Human Immunodeficiency Virus (HIV) that causes AIDS remained cloaked in a lack of awareness, cultural denial, fear, stigma, and resistance to preventive measures, brewing an epidemic. From the DRC, AIDS spread from central to East Africa to southern Africa and then to West Africa[xx].

The run-down isn't intended to invoke depression or misery but to encourage a deeper understanding of the magnitude of issues the continent has experienced and still experiences in the present day. To begin to really change its course, magical thinking won't work. It's beyond one person or group of persons, and long-term planning is fundamental. But we can borrow pages from successful examples in the far east. The four Asian Tigers of Singapore, Hong Kong, South Korea, and Taiwan were in similar straits to many African countries in the early 1960s and 1970s but transformed into industrialized, high-income economies from the 1990s into the 21st century. Due to its limited number of natural resources, one, in particular, is worthy of a special highlight, especially from the perspective of the individuals that led the historical initiative.

"We cannot afford to forget that public order, personal security, economic and social progress, and prosperity are not the natural order of things, that they depend on ceaseless effort and attention from an honest and effective government that the people must elect," wrote Lee Kuan Yew, the erstwhile and formidable leader of Singapore to a younger generation of Singapore in his autobiography 'From Third World to First: The Singapore Story 1965 –

2000.'

To this younger generation of Singaporeans that take the nation's prosperity and stability for granted, Lee writes about the challenges and struggles of taking his small country – bereft of natural resources and ravaged by war in 1942 followed by Japanese occupation – from one antagonized by surrounding "larger independent nations all pursuing nationalistic policies" to a world-class country and the most developed in Asia.

Again, while not perfect, Lee's life trajectory exemplifies many of the tenets this book espouses.

As a young man, Japan's occupation of Singapore exposed him to the cruelties fellow ethnicities can inflict on each other in the name of power or abuse thereof. Rather than adopt a defeatist mindset, the experience, according to him, strengthened his nationalistic identity and self-respect. Post-World War II, as a student in Britain, he was determined to be part of the leadership that would help put an end to British colonial rule in his country of origin. He returned to Singapore optimistic about his cause "but ignorant of the pitfalls and dangers that lay ahead.[xxi]"

Lee chronicles how he and his team worked against

"insuperable odds" to achieve prosperity from poverty in *three* decades:

> After grappling with the problem of unemployment for years since we first took office in 1959, all of us in the cabinet knew that the only way to survive was to industrialize. We had reached the limits of our entrepot trade. The outlook was a further decline. Confrontation with Indonesia was still on, and the Malaysians were determined to bypass Singapore. We cast around for solutions and were willing to try any practical ideas that could create jobs and enable us to pay our way. One of our soft drink manufacturers suggested to me that we promote tourism; it was labor intensive, needing cooks, maids, waiters, laundrymen, drycleaners, tour guides, drivers, and makers of souvenir handicrafts. Best of all, it required little capital.... To my relief, it did create many jobs and put coins into many empty pockets. It reduced but did not solve the unemployment problem.
>
> For that, we concentrated on getting factories started. Despite our small domestic market of 2 million, we protected locally assembled cars, refrigerators, air conditioners, radios, television sets, and tape recorders in the hope that they would later be partly manufactured

locally. We encouraged our own businesspeople who set up small factories to manufacture vegetable oils, cosmetics, mosquito coils, hair cream, joss paper, and even mothballs! And we were able to attract Hong Kong and Taiwanese investors to build factories for toys, textiles, and garments.

It was an unpromising start. The Jurong industrial estate in the west of Singapore was empty in spite of the vast sums we had spent on infrastructure. We had more than our share of failures.

Lee recounts one failure after another that it is quite difficult to imagine that the Singapore he speaks of is one that is steadfastly ranked among the most prosperous countries in the world, ahead of some of the same countries it once had to work hard to convince to invest in its potential. But with his dogged commitment and conviction that "the world does not owe us a living. We cannot live by the begging bowl," perhaps the Singapore we know of us today was inevitable. He was sure to lay the foundation early:

On my first official visit to America in October 1967, I recounted to 50 businesspeople at a luncheon in Chicago how Singapore had grown from a village of 120 fishermen in 1819 to become a metropolis of 2 million. This was because its philosophy was to provide goods and services "cheaper and better than anyone else, or perish." They responded well because I was not putting my hand out for aid, which they expect of leaders from newly independent countries. I noted their favorable reaction to my "no begging bowl" approach.

But it was far from a smooth sale, and Lee and his team had to redirect their efforts:

After several years of disheartening trial and error, we concluded that Singapore's best hope lay with the American multinational corporations (MNCs). When the Taiwanese and Hong Kong entrepreneurs came in the 1960s, they brought low technology, such as textile and toy manufacturing, which are labor-intensive but not large-scale. American MNCs brought higher technology in large-scale operations, creating many jobs. They had weight and confidence. They believed that their government was going to stay in Southeast Asia and their businesses were safe from confiscation or war loss.

I gradually crystallized my thoughts and settled on a two-pronged strategy to overcome our disadvantages. The first was to leapfrog the region, as the Israelis had done. This idea sprang from a discussion I had with a UNDP expert who visited Singapore in 1962. In 1964, while on a tour of Africa, I met him again in Malawi. He described to me how the Israelis, faced with a more hostile environment than ours, had found a way around their difficulties by leaping over their Arab neighbors who boycotted them to trade with Europe and America. Since our neighbors were out to reduce their ties with us, we had to link up with the developed world – America, Europe, and Japan – and attract their manufacturers to produce in Singapore and export their products to the developed countries.

The accepted wisdom of development economists at the time was that MNCs were exploiters of cheap land, labor, and raw materials. This "dependency school" of economists argued that MNCs continued the colonial pattern of exploitation that left the developing countries selling raw materials and buying consumer goods from the advanced countries. MNCs controlled technology and consumer preferences and formed alliances with their host governments to exploit the people and keep them down. Third World leaders believed this theory of neocolonialist exploitation, but [Goh] Keng Swee [the deputy prime minister] and I were not impressed. We had a real-life problem to solve and could not afford to be conscribed by any theory or dogma. Anyway, Singapore had no natural resources for MNCs to exploit. All it had were hard-working people, good basic infrastructure, and a government that was determined to be honest and competent. Our duty was to create a livelihood for 2 million Singaporeans. If MNCs could give our workers employment and teach them technical and engineering skills and management know-how, we should bring in the MNCs.

The second part of my strategy was to create a First World oasis in a Third World region. This was something Israel could not do because it was at war with its neighbors. If Singapore could establish First World standards in public and personal security, health, education, telecommunications, transportation, and services, it would become a base camp for entrepreneurs, engineers, managers, and other professionals who had business to do in the region. This meant we had to train our personnel and equip them to provide First World standards of service. I believed this was possible, that we could reeducate and reorientate our people with the help of schools, trade unions, community centers, and social organizations. If the communists in China could eradicate all flies and sparrows, surely we could get our people to change their Third World habits.

We had one simple guiding principle for survival, Singapore had to be more rugged, better organized, and more efficient than others in the region. If we were only as good as our neighbors, there was no reason for businesses to be based here. We had to make it possible for investors to operate successfully and profitably in Singapore despite our lack of a domestic market and natural resources.

The implementation of Lee's vision went beyond fancy marketing reports and projects; he also adopted a hands-on approach to convincing investors by ensuring that "the road from the airport to their hotel and office was neat and spruce, lined with shrubs and trees. When they drove into the Istana domain, they would see right in the heart of the city a green oasis, 90 acres of immaculate rolling lawns and woodland, and nestling between them, a nine-hole golf course. Without a word being said, they would know that Singaporeans were competent, disciplined, and reliable, a people who would learn the skills they required soon enough."

The approach worked with American investors who, in little time, overtook British, Dutch, and Japanese investments. By the late 1970s, Singapore had quelled its unemployment issues, made inadequate investment a thing of its past, and was laser-focused on keeping pace with innovative American manufacturing companies who, in 1997, numbered 200 in Singapore and valued at over $19 billion.

"If I have to choose one word to explain why Singapore succeeded, it is *confidence*," Lee said. It emboldened him to knit a delicate balance of creating partnerships and win-win alliances (including with former colonial powers) to help change the course of Singapore.

The combination of what he had learned from his education abroad and his faith in Singaporeans was imperative. However, he felt strongly that confidence was the key to Singapore's success story. It wasn't an arrogant type of confidence. It was of a healthier variety, borne out of the belief and knowledge that his constituents had talents that could be developed and that their collective talent was the "country's most precious asset."

Understanding that corruption would be the downfall of the

nation he was aspiring to create, Lee's leadership created an environment that frowned on and perceived it as a "threat to society." Having ethical people in office was fundamental to having an ethical government.

Just as importantly, rather than creating a government structure that was simply based on the platforms of Western powers, knowing his people, Lee cultivated his vision of what could most advance his country's development. For example, he did not believe democracy was the bedrock of development; rather, the emphasis on discipline would be more constructive.

Nor did Lee believe he and his team had all the answers. He realized that the outstanding success he now enjoys would be anchored on mindset. There would be highs and lows, he noted, using Singapore's then-strenuous relationship with Malaysia as an example:

> Singaporeans need to take these gyrations with equanimity, neither euphoric when relations are good nor despondent when relationships turn bad. We need steady nerves, stamina, and patience, while quietly standing up for our rights.

To him, leadership was beyond ability; it was a mix of

courage and determination to change things and stay the course even when the results of those changes proved tempestuous. When people observe these in a leader, alongside commitment, character, ability, activism, good judgment, and interpersonal skills, they are more apt to follow.

According to Lee, he and his team "never stopped learning because the situation kept on changing, and we had to adjust our own politics."

From the example of Lee's life and leadership, young African leaders can implement a variety of recommendations, such as always being on the lookout for opportunities to form alliances for the purpose of getting power that would be instrumental in effecting structural changes. Additionally, given the complexity of ethnic diversity in many African nations, these alliances ought to be built not just in political spheres but also across other socio-political spheres, including religion, secular groups such as unions and non-governmental organizations, and others.

While we actively seek these alliance-building opportunities, we must shy away from the zero-sum perspectives of our forebears that have created current enclaves of unnecessary strife and violence. The argument that these exist because colonial powers arbitrarily drew lines through the continent to create current-day countries, while historically accurate, is extremely limiting. And Africans' inability to sustainably mitigate these circumstances begs the question of why we remain committed to self-sabotaging conduct and pointing to the past for reasons why, as if solutions will magically materialize from there.

Additionally, by nature, zero-sum thinking focuses on immediate, temporary solutions that undermine long-term stability and success. Because you lose today, and you eagerly await your turn to "win" another day – by crook or force. But win-win scenarios mean most (the majority, if you will) have a stake in the situation at hand and minimizes the possibilities of violence from slighted or marginalized parties.

While Lee acknowledged the insight and sacrifices of his forebears, he wasn't afraid to pursue his team's vision. Young African leaders must keep this in mind because while we have an ethos of respecting elders because of their life experience – and rightfully so – we must make a distinction between this and respecting elders even when they are engaging in the wrong things that sabotage our collective future. To do so, we must challenge ourselves to higher levels of thinking, acting – and being. That includes seeing education as only what occurs within the walls of any institution. Every day you are alive, you are being educated, open your eyes, make connections others may miss, and apply what you learn. Employ critical thinking skills and stop taking things at face value.

To do so, let's change our mindset from being consumers to producers of philosophies. And if we must consume, let's consume quality products, services, and programming. We can learn from other parts of the world, but instead of striving to be replicas, we can learn to adapt principles and philosophies to African settings rather than wishing African countries are just like other societies or wondering why we experience failures from fitting a Western square peg into a round African hole.

Borrowing a page from Singapore's roadmap, African countries cannot continue to be destinations where other parts of the world come to scoop up raw materials and resources, process them and sell them back to Africans. Although we have made some strides in technology, we must pressure current and future leaders to diversify investments in various aspects of industry, particularly agro-processing, that convert the natural resources Africa is blessed with to semi-finished or finished products.

We must be willing to learn from other parts of the world, not from the standpoint of inferiority but from a place of exchanging ideas of worth. And remember to adapt such solutions to African settings. Explore how to create and benefit from the best of both worlds.

"No matter how full the river, it still wants to grow."

Congolese Proverb

Chapter 4:

The New Leaders We Need

If we heard it once, we have heard it a million times: poor political leadership is at the core of Africa's chronic underdevelopment.

There is a ton of evidence that many African (mis)leaders are profligates at the helm of corrupt administrations

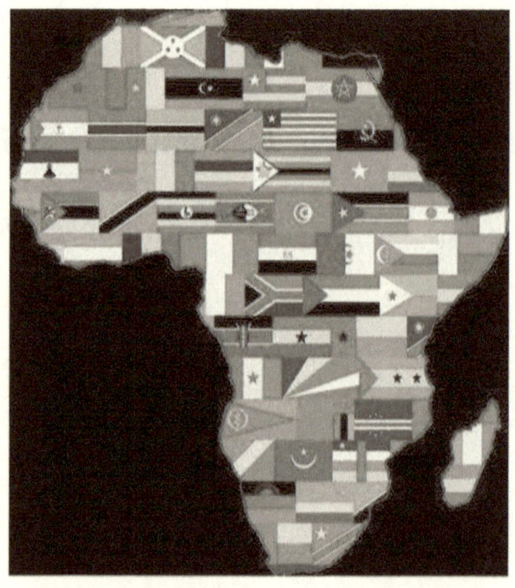

Figure 8: Map of African Flags. iStock

that pocket massive amounts of funds designated for social infrastructure investment. It is standard to point to corruption as the source of the gross underdevelopment on the continent. Of course, it plays a significant role, as does the colonial history that continues to affect the current reality on the continent on deep levels.

A less popular perspective would suggest everyday Africans also reexamine their self-image and recognize that leaders – the best and the worst of them – reflect the people. The reexamination might prompt certain uncomfortable observations that call into question whether the average African fundamentally believes they deserve a thriving functional society and a better self-image.

Have we conveniently reserved decent character as a value only politicians should possess while we ignore the deficit in character that plagues the continent?

Popular YouTube content creator Wode Maya traipses through the continent, shining the spotlight on bold, dynamic personalities that have accomplished feats defying the common belief that innovative ideas and successful business ideas cannot be wholly or largely implemented in Africa. In almost every one of his numerous endearing interviews, the response he receives to the question of what it would take to transform the continent, the responses have been consistent: change the mindset of the people to believe commercial success is possible despite the disheartening stereotypes. It's laudable advice and befitting of Maya's objective to contribute to changing the global perception of the continent.

However, present-day Africa needs a stronger foundation than external validation to make such success stories the norm instead of seemingly notable exceptions. New-era Africans hungry for change must be more intentional about the societal changes they would like to see.

A self-image repair necessitates a reassessment of the soil of our collective psyche to determine the type of psychic fruit we would like to bear going forward. It's time to reject powerlessness in a continent that has an abundance of resources. The Democratic Republic of the Congo is blessed with oil, diamonds, and gold; Nigeria has oil and ample agricultural products, and so does Ghana, Cote D'Ivoire is the world's leading producer and exporter of cocoa beans – just to name a few. Access to information has dramatically leveled the development playing field so that individuals' vision for a better continent can (and should) sooner materialize.

After all, individuals are the fabric of society. So, what kind of a continent (and country) do "you" envision? Can you imagine everything functioning as they should: quality schools for children (and not just for well-heeled families; affordable and consistent electricity, good roads, etc. A new mental constitution is critical to making such change possible, and young Africans would do well to make the shift from an overly outward-focused frame of reference, with a deep appetite for western standards, to an internal reference frame that seeks to transform the African continent by making the most of its vast natural and human resources.

As Africans invest in the technological capacity that creates a critical shift from the global natural resources exporter to processing more of its resources for local and foreign consumption, they won't need as much external aid. A track record of several decades has shown us that multinational good governance organizations seemingly well-meaning in their mission and objectives primarily address *symptoms* - the root is internal and runs deep. Multinational partners and private investors are never going to have Africans' best interest at heart more than Africans themselves and to expect otherwise is folly.

Young Africans' vibrant energies are better invested in being laser-focused on their areas of talent, developing a vision of what it will take to attain the highest possible level of success in those areas. For doctors, perhaps focus on creatively building partnerships that can help establish, amplify, or transform medical amenities. Farmers, what are some of the best international farming practices that are most adaptable to and suitable for your community? Each young adult focused on utilizing their talents in specific sectors benefits the entire national ecosystem sustainably and at a more rapid rate than waiting for African political leaders to create opportunities. The latter is yet to happen even after decades of complaints from their citizens and zero shame on the world stage as other international leaders and communities watch them squander their countries' resources.

There is a plethora of intellectuals, think tanks, and political pundits who regularly offer practical recommendations for more effective governance that are ignored just as often by politicians. But the reality is that we are all responsible for the stagnancy or growth of the continent. We must do the tough work of implementing the recommendations on individual scales too.

Consider, for example, the deep-rooted issue of corruption. Many Africans complain ad nauseam about its persistence but appear to haven't fully correlated the fact that the average person being comfortable with it is part of the reason there haven't been as significant strides made in curbing it.

As one Ghanaian columnist notes: "Political leaders bleeding their nations dry will not give us the whole story. If we only focus on the corrupt political leaders as development experts, media reports, and international partners do, we will certainly fail to understand the nature of the crisis engulfing our African continent. As we ignored in the past and continue to ignore the low-level bribes paid everywhere and daily on the continent, we're only going to see more corruption in the years ahead."[xxii]

While the practice of giving and receiving a bribe is fading slowly, more people would have to be fed up with it and be willing to take swifter and consistent action against it to bring about real change. Across the West, numerous Africans have developed a reputation for being smart, intelligent, and hardworking – this should be the case whether we are abroad or at home. Frankly, such energy is more critically needed on the ground in African countries. It shouldn't be an energy or ethos we tap into primarily when we deal with non-Africans or when we study or work abroad.

It's inevitable Africa will change, but "how" and "what" it will change into remains to be seen. There must be more collective intentionality behind its future. Yes, the continental brain drain is a reality. But it's disingenuous not to acknowledge that a significant amount of Africa's current (mis)leaders were educated in the West and other developed countries and worked extensively abroad in many cases. It's not enough to claim that too many of Africa's best minds are outside the continent when if those same minds returned, they would largely still have to assimilate into the current status quo to begin to make any substantive inroads in terms of impact. Or, to put it more bluntly, in many scenarios, they would almost have to dumb themselves down and dim their intellectual shine to even begin to engage on a meaningful level.

Rather than latching on to and utilizing their fresh, extensive, and oftentimes more innovative perspectives to move us as a collective forward, the often-unstated expectation is for them to revert to the very same standards we complain about and claim we so adamantly desire to change. The analogy of a dog chasing its own tail couldn't be clearer in understanding that reality lies both the answer and the challenge that Africa must repair itself from within.

What Does a Renewed Mindset Look Like?

The election period in many African countries usually comes with 'big man' politicians masquerading as the best choice for gullible masses. Even the incumbent, ignoring the mammoth promises they rode into office on (and never delivered), has a slew of reasons why they should be given another chance. In a show of fiscal responsibility to the public, previous presidential candidates in Nigeria and Liberia had promised to take pay cuts once elected but would subsequently be unable to account for a treasury that is significantly less robust than when they entered office. Others opt to valorize poverty, their election being the convenient time to recognize a significant percentage of the population they are surrounded by year-round are struggling and barely able to make ends meet. On one end of the extreme is a false identification with the masses, complete with as much of a show of asceticism as they can conceivably muster, and on the other are outright attempts to bribe the same populace they deem themselves qualified to lead with money or basic foodstuffs that would last perhaps a month or two tops. A viral video of a former Nigerian Senator and governorship aspirant put this on display when he encouraged state voters to make him governor because of his deep pockets. "If it's about money, I have brought loads of cash. The money is not only in naira; we have brought dollars, pounds sterling, Euro," he said. His comment drew wide criticism, but the fact he was comfortable making that statement as cell phones recorded shows the overall perception of voters.

To change the status quo that enables politicians to think so little of the average Nigerian, the populace must do away with thinking about themselves as not being capable of the leadership they seek. You are capable, and it's your time. You are one of the leaders you have been claiming you want to make your country better. You may not yet have the deep pockets or the social network of popular politicians, but you have your mind that can envision how your community can be transformed for the better. In many African countries, each election fever focuses heavily on the presidential race, but until there's a groundswell of quality leadership from the bottom up – in your local government council and in your state – little will change.

Until African youth at large adopt an accountability mindset that relentlessly pressurizes local government officials to use most of the funds allotted to their communities appropriately, local government community funds will continue to be siphoned into the personal bank accounts and private projects of so-called local government representatives.

More conscientious young leaders running for and supporting each other in local government positions – working in and living leadership as a service, not as a source of entitlement – is the potent force needed to change this reality.

You are neither helpless nor clueless about how to start making this a reality. If you are alive at this moment in time, it is because you deserve to be here. And if you are a young African that is eager to see a new dawn in your country and on the continent, you deserve to employ your imagination and take every action to contribute your part in regenerating the African collective.

"Knowledge without wisdom is like water in the sand."

Guinean Proverb

Chapter 5:

Moving Forward

More than 70 percent of Africa's 49 countries now have a startup tech hub that provides a critical digital and business infrastructure to a growing segment of technology and innovation-driven young minds.

Compared to the 1980s and early nineties, Africa is healthier, generally more peaceful, better educated, richer, and more democratic. Challenges persist, including a high rate of unemployment, widespread corruption, and gross underinvestment in physical infrastructure, but Africa is on the rise. Across the continent, there has been an explosion of artistic creativity, entrepreneurship, and scrappy tech-savvy innovation. [xxiii]

Young entrepreneurs profit from commercializing their ideas by providing community-based products and services.

In Ghana, social entrepreneur Fred Swaniker created the African Leadership Academy to groom thousands of young people in an immersive, servant leadership and entrepreneurship-based culture[xxiv]. The narrative is not just that of a change in demographics but of changing inherent conceptions as well. Young Africans are turning away from the legacies of past dictators such as Charles Taylor, Idi Amin, and Paul Biya, among others, and are willing to explore the servant leadership model of Nelson Mandela.

Every year, since its inception in 2014, nearly 5,800 young women and men from every country in sub-Saharan Africa are selected for the Mandela Washington Fellows of the Young African Leaders Initiative. The selection processes for these initiatives are rigorous as applicants are expected to have demonstrated leadership potential in tangible ways. With their record of accomplishments – as environmental activists, Paralympians, content creators, mental health pioneers, startup entrepreneurs, religious leaders, and more – these young leaders are a microcosm of a continent filled with talent and potential yet to be fully tapped. These young leaders present solutions to societal problems that stem from a deeper place than profit alone. For many, underneath the drive to innovate and their boundless creativity is the desire to secure a better life for themselves and their communities.

Here are some past and present examples of their resourcefulness:

- Sitawa Wafula from Kenya experienced traumatic sexual violence at the age of 18. She suffered from severe depression, which eventually resulted in a dual diagnosis of epilepsy and bipolar disorder. With rising medical bills and no support system, and little access to information, she endured the stigma of mental illness alone. She decided to channel her experience into helping others and started *My Mind, My Funk* Kenya's first free mental health resource hub that has blossomed and helped thousands of people.[xxv]

- Through her grandmother's experience with leprosy, Mabel Suglo from Ghana saw firsthand how individuals with physical disabilities are marginalized in daily life. Inspired by her grandmother's cleverness in creating make-shift shoes from used tires, Suglo set out to create the EcoShoes Project that would employ physically challenged and often-discriminated individuals to help her create quality, stylish shoes from discarded and recycled materials.[xxvi]

- When Satir Bahati of Rwanda lost his sight to glaucoma at the young age of 18, he sadly decided to forgo his dream of becoming a medical doctor or an engineer. Through Uwezo, he eventually actualized another dream: empowering disabled Rwandan youth with the tools and resources to lift them out of despair and into a sense of agency by advocating for and training these individuals for internships and, ultimately, permanent jobs.[xxvii]

- Munya Dodo is an award-winning journalist and founder of Zimbabwe-based social platforms that curate critical stories centered on strengthening democracy and government accountability. He trains young citizen journalists on using digital tools to raise awareness about socio-political challenges, including the country's response to the COVID-19 pandemic.[xxviii]

- Sherry Tumusiime from Uganda launched ZimbaWomen to provide full-service e-commerce services to women entrepreneurs and small and medium enterprises in the country and beyond.[xxix]

- Bethlehem Alemu of Ethiopia started soleRebels, the world's first Fairtrade Certified footwear by the World Fair Trade Organization. She started the business as a means of creating jobs for skilled but underemployed artisans and weavers that would help implement her vision of a cool, new twist on eco-friendly shoes for the Ethiopian market and beyond. Over 90 percent of the company's products are hand-made. Alemu has gone on to turn soleRebels into a global brand and is building others.[xxx]

There are many more examples of young Africans across the continent using technology and creative zest to address some of Africa's biggest challenges. In Zimbabwe, Maxwell Sangulani Chikumbusto invented the world's first green power generator.[xxxi] He also designed and built an electric vehicle that runs off radio frequencies to preserve fossil fuel and a hybrid helicopter capable of running on different types of fuels. In Nigeria, Hamzat Lawal developed a social transparency and accountability platform – Connected Development – to track government and international aid spending.

There is little doubt Africa is producing exceptional talent in the technology and entrepreneurship spheres. African youth can harness their gumption to tackle issues of governance too – an area where they are still starkly underrepresented.

Alliances Are Key

As legendary as Mandela's story was, he did not tackle apartheid alone. As a young revolutionary, he had veritable partners in people

Figure 9: Graffiti of Nelson Mandela. Pixabay

such as Thabo Mbeki, Walter Sisulu, Oliver Tambo, the venerable Desmond Tutu, and his charismatic then-wife Winnie Madikizela, among many others with whom he shared ideas and strategized to rescue the country from the grips of apartheid. So were the largest companies in the world today. Building alliances with fellow African leaders across the continent and in the diaspora who are willing to play a part in transforming the African continent for the better cannot be overstated. Young people can form groups to seek solutions to perennial societal concerns they face, including access to basic rights like clean water, quality education, health services, and more. Meetup groups are good avenues to connect, and so are Facebook, WhatsApp, and other platforms where individuals can discuss ideas, engage in constructive debate, and propose solutions to problems. Facebook, WhatsApp, Telegram, YouTube, and other sharing and message platforms also offer opportunities to connect with citizens from urban to rural communities to facilitate meaningful dialogue. A platform like TEDx is increasingly used for powerful storytelling and propagating intriguing perspectives and can be utilized more extensively. While social media offers opportunities to promote fresh ideas at lightning speed, traditional media – television, radio, newspapers – are still viable avenues to put and sustain a call for action by participating in talk show panels and organizing town hall meetings, letters to the editor and opinion articles to spotlight hot topics that directly impact constituents.

Navigating Ethnicity

The interrelation between African politics, democracy, and ethnicity is a complex one and one of the most significant problems currently faced by many African countries, from Sudan, Nigeria, and Rwanda, to South Africa and the list goes on. The continent is home to the most genetically diverse people on the planet.[xxxii] Africa has about 3,000 distinct ethnic groups and 2,000 languages. In most African countries, the candidacy of the average politician is dependent on ethnicity and religious sentiments rather than the substance of their platform. In fact, military coup leaders in the early 1980s and 1990s often cited, alongside political corruption and mismanagement of funds, ethnic differences as an underlying source of friction.

Understanding the historical antecedent of ethnicity in the continent is essential to understanding the complex role it plays in the socio-economic makeup of daily life, including political leadership. With decolonization came the largely arbitrary amalgamation of disparate tribes. In Nigeria, the British amalgamated the Igbos, Yoruba, and Hausas — three different, major tribes with little in common at the time. Favored by the British, the Hausas, based in the northern part of Nigeria, were the most represented in Nigerian politics. In Rwanda, Belgian colonial rule exacerbated friction between the Tutsi minority and the Hutu majority, bestowing power and status upon the former and fueling longstanding conflict and resentment that sparked the horrific genocide.

To navigate the intersectionality of ethnicity — compounded by religion — in leadership, some countries, such as Nigeria, established a de facto system for political candidacy from the presidential to local government levels that often pairs a Christian party nominee with a Muslim and vice versa. For presidential candidacy, each party also seeks nominees and running mates from different geopolitical zones to ensure firmer local representation and quell political tension that may arise because of real or perceived bias.

These types of multiethnic policies that recognize differences and promote cultural representation are not unfounded but are, in fact, necessary to fostering inclusion and furthering human development throughout the continent.

To lead in the continent, young African leaders need political and leadership appeal that cut across tribes, religions, and ethnic diversities. Because of institutions of culture, values, and strongly held ideologies, each tribe, religious and ethnic group take on increasing levels of significance. To effect sustainable change, young African leaders must not only stoke the sentiment as popular elections in Gambia, Ivory Coast, Burkina Faso, Liberia, Nigeria, and Ghana have done in prior years but communicate and execute their unique and concrete steps in actualizing the vision—and that part of the Venn diagram where the diversities intersect hold the keys to an accountable and inclusive government.

A Critical Cultural Shift

In African culture, respect, especially for elders, is held in the highest esteem. Ideal in theory, the deeply entrenched belief is counterproductive when young adults can never challenge authority regardless of how respectfully they do so. Young Africans are almost automatically labeled arrogant, rude, and disrespectful when they express differing perspectives about almost anything – family matters, societal ills, etc. It's a behavioral mode so ingrained that many young Africans may not fully appreciate how much it undermines their agency and future to respect so-called elders who are incapable of appreciating the intelligence, innovation, perspective, and creativity of other adults simply because they are younger. Beyond family dynamics, the practice extends to workplaces and the socio-economic-political halls of power. 'You must respect your elders' is a popular refrain, even when the elders are glaringly in the wrong.

For example, Iyabo Obasanjo, a former senator, and daughter of the former Nigerian president Olusegun Obasanjo wrote an open letter to her father in which she described his autocratic tendencies in both his political and familial affairs.[xxxiii] Public outcry labeled her a bastard and disgrace to womanhood – the decade-old letter recently resurfaced due to the former president's support for Peter Obi, who is deemed the shoo-in candidate in the 2023 election.[xxxiv] Few cultures, if any, would have celebrated Ms. Obasanjo's decision to air the family's dirty laundry in a major newspaper. In Nigeria, where younger Africans must walk a thin line between self-expression and reverence for the perspectives of their elders, her action was a complete cultural anathema.

The belief system is a monumental yet largely unaddressed hindrance against political progress, social justice, and human rights in the 21st century. It has contributed to disgraceful unaccountability in African countries and a stunted perception of leadership too many older African leaders are comfortable with embracing.

On the surface, young Africans may have tried to understand or explain away such a value system as a means of older African leaders keeping disruptive dissidents in check but feel largely disrespected and marginalized as a result. Why should African youth respect mis(leaders) that have looted countries they claim to lead dry, enriching their personal estates at the expense of the future of millions of young and unborn Africans? Increasingly frustrated and sidelined for too long, fortunately, young Africans are waking up. Youthful voices have ousted incumbent presidents and secured victory for new leaders in African countries. They have also been behind movements such as End SARs in Nigeria against police brutality that thrives where freedom of expression is too frequently stifled.

Africa deserves better leaders, and qualified, savvy, energetic young thinkers and doers deserve a seat at the table to hold their older counterparts accountable to all Africans. Leaders should earn respect based on the outcome of their actions. Sincere, self-aware, and self-respecting elders deserve to be honored and respected, but it's time Africans buried the reductive practice of respecting rogues and corrupt actors simply because of their chronological ages. They *do not* deserve it.

Social Media, Telecommunications Boon & Political Mobilization

When Gambia's dictator Yahya Jammeh refused to concede after suffering an electoral defeat to Adama Barrow in 2017, Salieu Taal created a hashtag #GambiaHasDecided that quickly gained traction and launched a movement that brought the international communities' attention to the political impasse, which eventually resulted in Jammeh's ouster after 22 years in office.[xxxv] Gambian youth's activism played a pivotal role in preserving the integrity of that election. Several years prior, Burkina Faso's former president Blaise Compaore started planning to change the constitution's term limits so he could seek a fifth term. Popular movements such as Ca Suffit (That's Enough) and Le Balai Citoyen (the Citizen's Broom) thwarted his efforts, marking the first time since the Arab Spring that popular movements managed to unseat an African president.

Today, tech-based strategies inform the quest for transparency and accountability in government. Shine Your Eye is a Nigeria-based SMS and web platform that facilitates public engagement with elected officials at all levels of government. Many presidents, including Uhuru Kenyatta of Kenya and Rwanda's Kagame, maintain active social media accounts aimed at making their presidencies more accessible. After Mugabe's ouster in 2017, newly installed President Emerson Mnangagwa began engaging Zimbabweans over social media, regularly posting videos and comments on Facebook to address citizen concerns and encouraging the public to message their thoughts. The use of social media as a platform to influence political change will only increase in the years ahead, and young leaders must harness it to build the future they will thrive in.

Mobile phone engagement is an unavoidable component of the change toolkit. The proliferation of mobile phone use in the continent in 2002 marked a critical juncture for innovation. At the time, one out of ten Africans owned a mobile. Nowadays, that number has escalated, especially in sub-Saharan Africa, where as many as nine in ten own mobile phones in South Africa. While smartphone usage is moderate so far, its growth is inevitable as mobile devices ensure access to online banking and social media.

Seventy percent of mobile money services in the world are in Africa, making it the fastest-growing mobile market globally.[xxxvi] Mobile technology has been a vital vehicle in delivering digital and financial inclusion in Sub-Saharan Africa.

The increasing number of internet users that have doubled and sometimes quadrupled in the past 10 years, has powered the trend. Benin, Sierra Leone, Niger, and Mozambique reflect the trend. In 2022, Nigeria had more than 80 million internet users, projected to climb to 117 million users by 2027 with its mobile-first market usage[xxxvii]; Egypt had more than 75 million[xxxviii]. The growing connectivity has made WhatsApp, YouTube, Facebook, Instagram, and Twitter the most-used social media platforms in the continent[xxxix], cementing the profiles of celebrities, political leaders, leading entrepreneurs, companies, and brands. The proliferation of mobile technology and social media powered by telecommunications growth has given average Africans the opportunity to influence and shape the opinions, mentality, and values of their followers. More young African leaders looking to shape their socio-political environment must fully leverage mobile technology to accomplish their specific objectives.

Blockchain as Potential Application for Social Change

Blockchain as an instrument of social change in the continent is untapped even as the popularity of the cryptocurrency for which it was invented, Bitcoin, grows despite past regulatory attempts to restrict its adoption.[xl] While the financial sector has proven to be a natural fit for blockchain, the tool can power digital transformation across sectors, including simplified and transparent governance. Could blockchain be the turning point for using technology to reduce corruption, unaccountability, and mismanagement in African governments? It remains to be seen, but it could provide the solutions to big problems – hyperinflation, high unemployment, fraudulent real estate transactions, tax evasions, mismanagement of public funds, etc. – that plague many countries. Blockchain can reduce corruption and foster a high level of accountability in governance when government officials know that transactions are captured in a decentralized, validated, and verifiable format. Similarly, where African governments have a big problem with data acquisition, analysis, and storage, blockchain can facilitate sound policy decisions, which governments need and can use big data to make. For example, with blockchain, the identity and information of citizens can be captured and linked for accurate census counts that inform efficient infrastructure investment. Young African leaders of tomorrow may not be able to completely eradicate mismanagement and embezzlement of public funds, but they are at an advantage when it comes to applying technology to bolster transparency and accountability; blockchain can help.

Music as a Tool for Transformation

Africa's new generation of performers are taking their sound to all corners of the globe, riding the popularity of Afropop with a commandingly infectious sound that is less about social consciousness and increasingly about creating trailblazing African beats heavily influenced by Hip Hop. With its requisite braggadocio and celebration of the trappings of financial success, the formula is working, and Nigeria seems to have the lion's share of the growth. Today, Burna Boy, Wizkid, and Davido, three of Nigeria's biggest Afropop stars, are more popular than many world leaders, selling out major international entertainment venues such as New York's Madison Square Garden and London's O2 Arena in record time. Previously, only entertainers such as Beyonce, Rihanna, Rolling Stones, and Spice Girls could boast of such feats. It may be unrealistic to expect the unprecedented commercial success of today's Afropop music to give way to what might be considered more socially conscious music that takes unwavering stances about corruption, nepotism, and other societal ills. But music has proven to be an agent of social change in the continent in years past. The name recognition of legends such as Fela Anikulapo Kuti, Miriam Makeba, Angelique Kidjo, Lucky Dube, and more almost stem as much from their incredible talent as their uncanny ability to fuse substantive narratives of social and political consciousness into their remarkable melodies. Kuti's original, unafraid, eccentric Afrobeat revolutionized music in Nigeria from the 1970s through the early 1990s, with friends and foes dancing to irresistible tracks that strongly rebuked military dictatorship and castigated corrupt (mis)leaders. Further back, South African composer Vuyisile Mini composed the protest song "Ndodemnyama we Verwoerd" (Beware, Verwoerd), which became one of the most popular songs in the nation. With his soulful compositions, he emerged as one of the most powerful organizers of the resistance against apartheid.

As in yesteryears, there is room and appetite for both, and there are more recent examples to support that. Bobi Wine's popularity as a Ugandan singer and actor catapulted him from a self-described "Ghetto King" to a Member of Parliament in 2017, securing the seat from the ruling opposition party. At 36, his growing fame ensured election victories for several can-

Figure 10: An EndSARS Protest in Lagos
Kaizenify/Wikimedia

didates he backed the next year. He fast became a political threat to the long-time president, Museveni, whom he faced head-on in a highly contentious 2021 general election.

Inspired by Childish Gambino's audacious satirical 2018 hit "This is America," Nigerian rapper and actor Falz turned a critical gaze on the country's social justice shortcomings with an emphasis on corruption and police brutality. The popular song, which the government attempted to censure, would eventually become a rallying tune for youth protesting the #EndSARS in Lagos. Falz galvanized top performers and celebrities to demand accountable policing from the government. Attempting to ban the politically charged "This is Nigeria" only served to reinforce its message internationally. Kenya's chart-topping Afropop group Sauti Sol had a similar realization. The band rose to fame with numerous party favorites. But their soulful ode "Tujiangalie" reflects on present-day Kenya rife with political corruption, social division, infatuation with materialistic frivolities, and in a questionable state since its independence.

In the Sigauque Project, a band based in Maputo, Mozambique, artists come together to make a difference through their music, weaving pertinent messages about xenophobia, women's issues, resilience in the face of what appear to be insurmountable odds, and more.

The opportunity and responsibility to promote social change is ample in African music. Music is integral to African culture and heritage and has proven to be an effective unifier, evident in the rate at which young artists from across the continent collaborate. Followed by a gazillion adoring fans, the influence of African music stars has made them influential ambassadors and advocates for accountable African governments. The creative energy artists, songwriters, and musicians employ to produce the pulsating hits that vibrate in nightclubs around the world or stir happy vibes at social events can also inspire songs that uplift messages about socio-political and economic change.

There is room for music to not just capture the plight and concerns of the less fortunate in African societies but one that employs the repetitive power of music to strum up and inspire possible solutions. And it won't entirely be to an altruistic end either; less corrupt, functional, and fiscally responsible governance shores up their continued commercial successes.

Channeling Uprisings for Long-Term Change

In recent years, uprisings in the continent have been occurring at a greater frequency. Whether to protest a particular issue or broader political change, the events are indicative of growing intolerance for so-called "leaders" that abuse their power. And to add insult to injury strive to stay in office for much, much longer than the constitution permits – essentially perceiving their time in office as that of a monarchy. The protests – and commensurate hashtags - against such anti-good government moves are instrumental in raising awareness about the demands of the people and sharing best practices for effective campaigns. However, Africa has a long history of uprisings, and while the indignation over dictator-style governance is valid, movements built around being anti 'a specific personality in office' or a specific administration undermine long-term impact. Securing Africans' access to basic infrastructure such as clean water, education, healthcare, clean, safe road networks, and electricity transcend the cult of personality that is synonymous with African government administrators. As young leaders explore and employ more creative social media tactics to mobilize change, their approach must be anchored on the deeper issues at play and not focused on removing an individual from office. For example, say dictator-style leader 'X' or corrupt leader 'Z' is successfully removed from office due to social pressure – protests, successful social campaigns – then what? A different president or governor or whoever is elected or selected via party politics. Another four or eight years go by with minimal, if any changes, that are typically limited to a specific or a couple of pet project initiatives. Since African leaders have historically failed to respond effectively to general demands for good governance, young African leaders must craft social campaigns that are deeply issues-based, prioritized, and accompanied by a systemic framework that outlines how the demands can be met and relevant metrics to gauge effectiveness. It is not enough to continue to demand 'power supply' or 'good public schools' while tangible and important issues are too vague, and African politicians, with only a few notable exceptions, make all the promises they can muster and seldom come close to delivering on even a fraction of them.

In a valuable explainer, the policy institute Chatham House surveyed international mass movements for political change before and during the 2020 pandemic lockdowns[xli]. The piece discusses key elements of impactful protest, with ten insightful recommendations such as prioritizing meaningful dialogue, clearly communicating demands, encouraging citizen action in schools, and combining all non-violent protest mechanisms. These suggestions have the makings of a solid foundation for young African leaders to proceed further, distilling their demands (and vision) for change into a framework that benchmarks success criteria and serves as an accountability mechanism.

"There are no shortcuts to the top of the palm tree."

Cameroonian Proverb

Chapter 6:

Finding Answers Within

Since time immemorial, people have migrated to various parts of the earth in search of better opportunities. In fact, in addition to homo sapiens being traced to Ethiopia, historical records also trace the first migration to the African continent.[xlii] Present-day immigration continues worldwide, and African countries are no exception. Just as Africans immigrate to other parts of the world, major cities in the continent also receive an influx of immigrants from other parts of the world, taking advantage of business opportunities to tap into the vast markets in these cities. While it's normal for many Africans to seek better pastures, it's a reasonable assertion that not every smart, ambitious young African is destined to only realize their full potential abroad. If everyone leaves, who will develop your country? Borrowing a page from the business immigrants who seek opportunities in, say, Nigeria, a country many Nigerians are eager to "japa" from, i.e., desert on any given day. Even in such a tough, competitive terrain, many business-minded immigrants prioritize all the possibilities the country offers over the myriad of challenges that come with living and doing business in Nigeria.

Nonetheless, surviving and thriving will require shifting from a mindset of being employed where quality, traditional employment opportunities are few to a producer mindset that creates products and services and potentially hires others down the line. It will require learning a marketable skill one can transact in person or online and on various platforms. Young African leaders can identify and explore such opportunities

Figure 11: A young child models Mandela

by embracing and developing their competencies, intelligence, and turning inward for their inspiration, and displaying requisite confidence in all their knowledge and growth. Enough of overly diverting your unique attention and power to religion and the outward-focused psyche that someone (or something) external should or is coming to rescue us. While the legacy of too many African (mis)leaders pales in comparison to Mandela's, whose powerful legacy cannot be replicated, his leadership style emphasized the role of everyone in transforming South Africa and the rest of the African continent. Perhaps he recognized that just as there could never be another him, there can never be another you. So, it would be futile to try to lead in the exact manner Mandela led. However, there's little doubt his servant leadership approach would likely be best in most situations, given African countries' problematic bouts with despotic rule. It is clear from Africans' experience with (mis)leaders that next-generation African leaders can abhor the blatant outrage of inequity that plague many of the continent's countries.

It will also mean being more discerning and discriminating with our collective power of the tongue. As we slowly but surely make the change into transformative leadership in Africa – yes, things can't and won't remain the same forever – ought to come greater recognition that the persistent criticism that is frequently dispersed and tapped into about your country of origin only serves as a self-fulfilling prophecy instead of a solution-oriented reality. The sustained diatribe of all that's wrong with or bad in Africa primarily and unwittingly affirms what we say we don't want. And since scientific studies[xliii] have established how powerful thoughts are a colossal waste of our collective psychic intent.

Ripples of Change

Nigeria's 2023 election is one of its most talked about in decades[xliv]. The primary contenders represent parties that many consider standard bearers of the old guard, i.e., more of the same corrupt politicians or more forward-thinking candidates that can potentially implement systemic changes. Young voters are drawing a line in the sand with a strong 'enough is enough' stance against party politics and priorities usurping basic good governance. Unequivocally, Peter Obi, the erstwhile governor of Anambra state, is the candidate they have thrown their support behind. At 61, the soft-spoken Obi, who prided himself on fiscal responsibility during his tenure as a state leader, appears to be a breath of fresh air for younger and older Nigerians alike who believe they now have a qualified candidate who can help begin to tackle Nigeria's elephantine issues. But Obi is one individual; expecting him to be or wave the magic wand that will set a dismally performing government aright is unrealistic. But the excitement surrounding Obi is constant and contagious. Even beyond Nigeria's shores, the Obi and "Obidient" phenomenon is undeniable. Almost eerily, it harkens back to another political sensation that almost 30 years ago attempted to wrestle Nigeria out of then-military rule to democratic leadership: Moshood Kashimawo Olawale Abiola. After winning the fateful June 12, 1993, presidential election, MKO was systemically denied the opportunity to assume the role. He died several years later after he was released from prison, where he had been incarcerated for refusing to relinquish his undeniable claim to a presidency he had handily won. Numerous

Figure 12: M.K.O Abiola.
Fhssupdate.blogspot.com

Nigerians desired for MKO to become president. Until the end, MKO also believed justice would prevail. Unfortunately, it didn't, for the legendary international business tycoon who was renowned for his unabashedly big, generous heart. Not even the years of fostering goodwill through his philanthropic donations and friends in the highest of places in Nigeria and abroad could correct the blatant wrong of denying the presidency to its rightful winner. It seemed the entire world was watching as the dream of millions of Nigerians was flung to the ground, stepped on, and coldly crushed into the earth bit by bit. MKO paid the ultimate price, as did Kudirat Abiola, his senior wife at the time, who had actively campaigned on his behalf and launched a pro-democracy movement upon his imprisonment. Many everyday Nigerians who dared to protest and demand justice also lost their lives.

One of the many lessons we can draw from their lives of conviction and dedication to a cause greater than themselves is a realization that effective governance cannot lie on one person's shoulders, and that includes Obi's genteel shoulders. Since the political pendulum swings in different directions based on circumstantial factors, African youth must not let the preference for, or love of any candidate imperil their countries. If Africa must achieve its enormous potential, then African youth must focus on learning how to agree to disagree and peacefully coexist with disparate ethnic, religious, and ideological persuasions.

Outlining a New Leadership Framework

Term limits often arise when discussions about governance come up in African countries. However, regular transfer of power, as seen in countries such as Ghana, Nigeria, Botswana, and Mauritius, has not translated to massive transformation. Apparently, it's hardly a panacea to continental leadership ills. Nonetheless, regular transfer of power provides the citizenry a chance to at least hope for, if not look forward to, new policies and programmatic initiatives the incoming administration plans to adopt. There is growing urgency surrounding raising awareness across platforms to educate and enlighten the populace on the power they have in the governance process. Several years ago, Samson Itodo, a young Nigerian community organizer and convener of the #NotTooYoungToRun, tapped into that momentum to launch a successful two-year advocacy campaign that led to the passage of the landmark bill that lowered the age of candidacy for the presidency from 40 to 35 and in the House of Representative and Senate from 30 to 25. The United Nations, African Union, and ECOWAS also adopted the campaign on a broader scale. Itodo's courage and innovation with #NotTooYoungToRun is worth emulating across the continent. He is one example of how young African leaders can change the systemic framework in ways that categorically affect their lives and persevere to accomplish a goal despite seemingly insurmountable obstacles. Such persistence fosters novelty, imagination, and creativity that will yield new and better goals, ideas, and solutions to problems. The world needs great leaders who not only charismatically spew great rhetoric but put forth action behind their words — the need is dire in the African continent.

"To be free is not merely to cast off one's chains, but to live in a way that respects and enhances the freedom of others."

Nelson Mandela

Chapter 7:

Some Steps in the Right Direction

Even with the enormity of the challenges on the continent, some African countries are making significant strides fueled by innovation and buoyed by resourcefulness. Both Rwanda and Namibia have made great inroads in healthcare, with the former leading in the IT revolution – a remarkable achievement since the country was practically offline just over a decade ago. In Rwanda, community-based health insurance, community health workers, and good external partnerships have resulted in the highest decline in maternal and child mortality rates ever recorded in the country[xlv]. Technology has played a critical role in access to healthcare as drone aircrafts quickly deliver blood and medical supplies to rural hospitals. The nation has also seen an increase in the network base of volunteer community health workers in villages across the country serving as links to health facilities.

In addition to becoming an East African IT hub, Rwanda is also tapping into its potential to be a financial services hub. Ghana, Kenya, and Morocco are other countries that have also gained mileage in universal health coverage implementation. Tanzania has developed a reputation for thrifty governance. These are obviously just a few examples, and in that summary emphasis has been placed on the outcomes of these leadership initiatives

Figure 13: Winhoek, Namibia

than on the leaders who orchestrated them to highlight the significance of the vision. It's one thing to know what needs to be done to make African communities better; it's another to implement the steps to make things happen – vision is what bridges the gap. Support current leaders that have it, cultivate it in younger leaders, get clear(er) on yours and let it be compelling enough to drive you.

After briefly exploring some countries that are trending towards success on the continent, the following are individual and collective level suggestions to spark ideas that can stimulate change on the continent. These tips are not law but are outlined to encourage a new(er) perspective on *being* and *acting* on the continent.

So, here we go:

The Individual

- **Remember that leadership is not "out there" or only to be found in other, more accomplished, eloquent, or attractive people.** It also doesn't mean you have to be uber extroverted or must be in the spotlight or even pedestalized.

- **Decide what kind of leader you would like to be.** Your ability to incorporate the above into daily life will stem from knowing your personality type, leadership style, and the subject matter areas that are most important to you. The servant leadership style has been espoused in this book because it most engages participants, providing more opportunity for everyone to do their part, and typically doesn't concentrate power on the leader. Africans have already had a long history of autocratic (mis)leadership to realize it's not effective.

- **Cultivate a stronger self-image.** It's no secret that Africans are some of the most outward-looking people. It's obvious in our willingness to quickly emulate the lifestyle and fashion trends from external cultures. But if we are going to be so eager to copy, let's copy all the way and copy all the good things perceived as "better" in these societies, including the hard, visionary, and intentional work of building stronger governmental frameworks, community infrastructure, and stronger government accountability systems. While we are at it, let's strive to create trends others follow – that come from a place of more authenticity and power. It shows you like and appreciate you for you and what you bring to this world, not unwittingly and constantly valuing and ingesting what others produce – image, lifestyle products, etc.– while looking down on what you create (or can create). It's not wise to continue to give away our power and incredulously wonder why the second-class perception and treatment of Africans internationally can't seem to shake. Take inventory of the perceptions you have of yourself (and others that look like you), the products you consume, and where you currently direct your valuable time, attention, energy, and money. There's nothing wrong with an unwavering positive self-image. In fact, it can be considered the basis of a healthy mental state. The truth is others that we have been overly eager to imitate have been very intentional about cultivating a superlative self-image of themselves – as they should; this is not intended to malign any group – so much so that they have convinced you to set yours aside and endlessly pursue theirs. Only Africans can, of course, correct that unfortunate phenomenon.

- **Shun outdated tribal, ethnic, and religious divisions.** Enough said. Thankfully, change is in motion here but apparently not fast enough, and so it bears repeating here. Many Africans still don't see through the veil of how these three are used to sow discord, create havoc, incite violence, and distract the collective from the activities and outcomes of mis(leadership). Refuse to fall for the ruse by making a conscious decision to not negate others simply because of their tribal, ethnic, and religious affiliations. Encourage others in your familial and social circles not to do the same.

- **Let cooler heads prevail.** Too many videos have

circulated online of supposed "leaders" engaging in brawls in the House of Representatives and in parliament. Ahead of Nigeria's February 2023 elections, such disgraceful behavior has even extended to the campaign trail, with some campaign supporters physically attacking and maiming opponents' supporters. With other important elections on the horizon in Sierra Leone, Liberia, and the Democratic Republic of the Congo, young Africans must recognize emotional intelligence goes a lot further than the use of brute force. Effectively leading any campaign or group in Africa is not for the faint of heart, but that doesn't give anyone the right to resort to violence to get their point across or force their opinions on others with differing perspectives. Leading is not a zero-sum game, so it's critical to know one's strengths and weaknesses to be in greater command of your emotional state. It is your responsibility, and plus, it's necessary to generate the potent, positive energy any campaign or movement requires in building the strong, mutually beneficial relationships that bring people with often divergent views together in the pursuit of a shared goal. Giving into the use of brute force at the slightest provocation is the poster child of how *not* to lead.

- **Be adaptable.** Almost self-explanatory but still worth mentioning. Beyond the ability to lead, it will take a mix of courage and determination to implement meaningful changes and stay on course even when such changes may seemingly be unruly. Along with good character, activism, sound judgment, interpersonal skills, and other qualities that make a good leader, adaptability is a must-have. The greatest leaders never stop learning because they recognize situations are ever-changing, and one must be flexible enough to adjust their own approach, politics, perspective, etc.

The Collective

- **Think, act, and "be" different.** We can't continue to be so-called independent in words alone yet dependent in our realities. Enough of empty, sugar-coated promises come election time. Enough of the same results that have only made most Africans destitute, desolate, deformed, and divided. It's clear Africans must show up differently as a collective if we must achieve a different result as a continent. It is time to say no to politics and ideologies that have wrecked life opportunities for constituents. No to tribalism-based angst that has led to needless wars and ethnic conflict. It is time to find a sense of purpose in our hearts as a collective to seek the peace that will ensure unity among the people amid immense cultural diversity.

- **Encourage divergent perspectives and merge them.** Instead of being so ready to let differing perspectives deteriorate into conflict, find a middle ground. Communities consist of individuals with varied interests, perspectives, priorities, and aspirations. But there's always some kind of middle ground, be curious and patient enough to find and use it to bridge differences. Fundamentally, recognize that a correct self-image can also enable more Africans to appreciate each other as worthy of their own perspectives, visions – and simply being. Let's not obliterate this basic right out of willful ignorance, poor self-image, and arrogance. Utopia doesn't exist, but functional, thriving communities can (and do). Distill the best ideas that emerge from your environment, prioritize them, and utilize implementing them as an opportunity to enhance harmony, not foment disunity.

- **Stop concentrating the concept of leadership on one person.** Election after election finds many Africans raising their hopes that the next president will be the answer to their prayers and "rule" them better than the previous. As discussed in the preceding pages, not enough emphasis is placed on holding grassroots leadership accountable. Beyond the political sphere, such a stance is crippling because it perpetually externalizes good leadership in someone or something other than within ourselves and fosters the domestic (not to mention international) perception of constituents as helpless victims. That is not a true or complete picture and does absolutely nothing to drive impactful change. How can constituents work together to implement the changes they want to the best of their abilities while still finding and sustaining ways to hold their local and national governments accountable in a more empowering posture? Frankly, versions of answers to that question have been what has held many African communities together thus far in the face of horrible governance. Systematizing such approaches while putting consistent pressure on the government as a collective to "serve" the needs of the people and not "rule" over them can help.

- **Only support leaders with a vision and actual plan(s).** As a collective, we can't say we desire change and keep falling for the same formula. Politicians and empty promises go together; it's the reason many people all over the world are increasingly disillusioned with political elections and overall political processes. If you choose to partake, support candidates that not only state all the right words but have a vision and *actual* plans to back it up. Push them to make realistic, tangible projections. Anyone can make campaign promises, but *how* they plan to accomplish these promises is what we want. Be uncompromising with your demand – and honoring your basic right – that they deliver actual plans, not broad strokes of promises to snag your vote. It doesn't guarantee they will deliver, but it surely communicates voters are tired of sweet-sounding but deceptive promises.

- **The grass isn't always greener outside.** With the

growing number of YouTube videos by Africans and immigrants of Afro descent sharing their insight on living in the West, more people are realizing that fact. It is prompting some to move back to their African country of origin or other countries in the continent for a variety of reasons. Some who have completed their higher education are tired of the work-around-the-clock rat race, while others crave the familiarity of being back in (or close to their hometowns) where the question 'where are you from?' doesn't feel like a real or perceived slight that reinforces being 'other', yet others because of their spiritual awakening. Nonetheless, whether within or outside of the African continent, many keep up with news from their countries, while others are more hands-on in contributing in their unique ways to make life better for others at home. The decision to migrate elsewhere permanently or temporarily is a personal one. For the young leaders who have chosen to relocate to their countries of origin and are looking to make tangible contributions, recognize that the solutions to Africa's problems lie within, not outside of it. While the task of transforming a nation and continent is too monumental for one person (with all the supposed power presidents wield, not even they can accomplish it alone), stop thinking the impact you can make is too small. It's time to turn a new page and key into a new narrative. Imagine for a few minutes how much of a game-changer it would be if every young African adopted such a mindset. Now, do and own your part.

- **Shift from mindless consumption.** Never at any point in history has it been easier to acquire goods and services from around the world. Although some of the largest consumers of these accoutrements of modern life, including luxury products, Africans are barely manufacturers of these items, even though the continent is the source of the raw materials used to produce them. Desiring the comfort and the quality these purchases afford is understandable, so should being more mindful of the global socio-economic implications of mindlessly supporting and financing such travesty (See *Cultivate a stronger self-image under Individual framework* above too). It should give Africans pause why we are so content with the continent's natural resources – even oil and food staples – being used to manufacture products that are then sold at a premium back to us. Of course, there's an understanding here that the policies (mis)leaders endorse created and contribute to the conundrum. But setting aside national coffers for a moment, we (you and I) control our individual and collective wallets and purses. Understanding the power they wield means having a deeper appreciation for the irony of driving luxury cars through pothole-filled, thrash strewn-roads or of wearing luxury fashion to traipse across open smelly sewage-flowing gutters. 'I don't like beautiful things,' said no one ever in the history of the world. Hardly an admonition, the recommendation here is to stop and think of our consumption more wholistically and to make more of an effort to prioritize products that uplift our collective image and contributions to the world.

Conclusion:

Leading in a "Non-Traditional" Era

A demographic of more than 70% under the age of 30 means out-of-the-box thinking is needed in the African continent to challenge inept governance, influence election outcomes, and assure ethical leadership. Fortunately, new generation Africans have experienced and are gradually moving away from the stifling mindset that *selfish, irresponsible* leaders that are leaving behind fiscally abusive, bankrupt legacies must be respected no matter what at the cost of future generations of Africans – a cost that is just too great. There's proof of what hasn't worked all around you, so don't let anyone continue to gaslight you with the same washed-up "solutions" and "plans" that will have your community in the same state (or worse) 10 years from now. All over the continent, a growing number of young people are eager for change. They recognize the influence of social media mobilization and aren't afraid to wield it. But to really move things forward, that command is slowly but surely extending to more grassroots activity and representation. A shift from criticizing the (mis)leaders will have to give way to having the agency to put forth actual leadership proposals, meaning we will have to step into the responsibilities of creating, embodying, and implementing the leadership we yearn to experience on the continent. Some of the avenues outlined in this book may inspire ideas you have always thought of bringing to life, or perhaps you know other young(er) people with great ideas and would rather partner with them. Either way, use all the legitimate resources and skills at your disposal to realize your vision of turning disappointments into tangible solutions. More than just being formally educated leaders, the continent needs leaders whose heads to serve are in sync with their hearts. People who are open to taking on new challenges and trying new things while fully exploring instead of shunning homegrown solutions that address the unique realities of their local communities. It's truly exciting that if they opt to take on the challenge, their time has finally come.

Author's Biography

Ufuoma Otu uses her multidisciplinary communications and project management skills to secure favorable outcomes for wide-ranging clients when she's not pondering solutions to societal issues. Her writing and communications campaigns have received numerous awards, including PR News, Public Relations Society of America, International Association of Business Communicators, and Hermes Creative Awards. A certified Professional Scrum Master, she is a big proponent of the servant leadership style with which she has led cohesive project teams. She loves delicious international hand pies and is often looking forward to sampling the next most flavorful one.

Endnotes

[ii] Africa Union, "Youth Development," January 20, 2021, available at: https://au.int/en/youth-development

[ii] John Burke, "Young Africans: New Wave of Politicians Challenges Old Guard," The Guardian, September 21, 2018, available at: https://www.theguardian.com/world/2018/sep/21/young-africa-new-wave-of-politicians-challenges-old-guard

[iii] Nelson Mandela, "I dream of an Africa which is in peace with itself," Good Reads, available at: https://www.goodreads.com/quotes/182049-i-dream-of-an-africa-which-is-in-peace-with

[iv] John C. Maxwell, "The 21 Indispensable Qualities of Leader: Becoming the Person Others Will Want to Follow, September 1, 2007, available at: https://a.co/d/7z6tQ2s

[v] Niccolò Machiavelli, "The Prince," February 21, 2021, available at: https://amzn.to/3IEdNcw

[vi] Toby Shapshak, Almost All Of Facebook's 139 Million Users In Africa Are On Mobile," Forbes, December 18, 2018, available at: https://www.forbes.com/sites/tobyshapshak/2018/12/18/almost-all-of-facebooks-139m-users-in-africa-are-on-mobile/?sh=7995792c68e7

vii Datareportal, "YouTube Statistics and Trends," August 15, 2022, available at: https://datareportal.com/essential-youtube-stats

viii Datareportal, "Twitter Statistics and Trends," August 22, 2022, available at: https://bit.ly/3k7tkYi

ix Jessica Eggert, "The Africa that the media never shows you," Mashable, July 7, 2015, available at: https://mashable.com/archive/the-africa-media-never-shows-you

x Tofe Ayeni, "Rwanda: President Kagame says he may run for 4th term in 2024," The Africa Report, July 12, 2012, available at: https://www.theafricareport.com/222337/rwanda-president-kagame-says-he-may-run-for-4th-term-in-2024/

xi Yanditswe, "Rwanda among the 4 least corrupt countries in Africa - TI Report," Rwanda Broadcasting Center, January 24, 2020

xii Kennedy Elliott, "Rwanda's legislature is majority female. Here's how it happened," National Geographic, October 15, 2019, available at: https://www.nationalgeographic.com/culture/graphics/graphic-shows-women-representation-in-government-around-the-world-feature

xiii Takudzwa Hillary Chiwanza, "Here is How Rwanda Became Africa's Cleanest Country," The African Exponent, August 14, 2020, available at: https://www.africanexponent.com/post/7774-here-is-how-rwanda-became-africas-cleanest-country

xiv Richard Grant, "Paul Kagame: Rwanda's redeemer or ruthless dictator?" The Telegraph, July 22, 2010, available at: https://www.telegraph.co.uk/news/world-news/africaandindianocean/rwanda/7900680/Paul-Kagame-Rwandas-redeemer-or-ruthless-dictator.html

[xv] Id.

[xvi] Id.

[xvii] Martin Meredith, "The Fate of Africa: A History of Fifty Years of Independence," January 1, 2005, available at: https://a.co/d/2DfmPma

[xviii] Id.

[xix] Id.

[xx] Id.

[xxi] Lee Yuan Yew, "From Third World to First: The Singapore Story 1965 – 2000," October 3, 2000, available at: https://a.co/d/govVDtB

[xxii] Nana Kwaku M Asamoah, "Corruption In Africa – The Crisis of Our Time?," Africa.com, June 20, 2019, available at: https://www.africa.com/corruption-in-africa-the-crisis-of-our-time

[xxiii] Fade Ogunro, "Creating employment in Africa's creative industry through technology," May 15, 2019, available at: https://guardian.ng/technology/creating-employment-in-africas-creative-industry-through-technology

[xxiv] Abiodun Ajayi, "Fred Swaniker: A Social Entrepreneur with A Big Vision," Africa OTR, December 12, 2020, available at: https://africaotr.com/fred-swaniker-a-social-entrepreneur-with-a-big-vision

[xxv] Doris Njoki, "Who is Sitawa Wafula: Kenya's BET Award winner," Mpasho, June 29, 2022, available at: https://mpasho.co.ke/exclusives/2022-06-29-who-is-sitawa-wafula-kenyas-bet-award-winner

[xxvi] How Africa News, "Meet Mabel Suglo, The Ghanaian Shoe Manufacturer Who's Helping Disabled Artisan to Turn Trash into Eco-friendly Footwear," May 3, 2017, available at: https://howafrica.com/meet-ma-

bel-suglo-the-ghanaian-shoe-manufacturer-whos-helping-disabled-arti-sans-to-turn-trash-into-eco-friendly-footwear

[xxvii] Anna Leach, Naomi Larrson and Katherine Purvis, "10 activists changing lives for disabled people around the world," The Guardian, June 22, 2016, available at: https://www.theguardian.com/global-devel-opment-professionals-network/2016/jun/22/10-activists-changing-lives-disabled-people-around-world

[xxviii] The Movement Hub, "Munyaradzi Dodo: My Journey," November 12, 2020, available at: https://www.themovementhub.org/stories/muny-aradzi-dodo-my-journey-into-digital-activism

[xxix] Rebecca Rwakabukoza, "This all-woman team is helping other fe-male entrepreneurs in Uganda adopt new tech," One, January 19, 2017, available at: https://www.one.org/us/blog/this-all-woman-team-is-help-ing-other-female-entrepreneurs-in-uganda-adopt-new-tech

[xxx] Justin Probyn, "The Journey so far: Bethlehem Tilahun Alemu, founder, soleRebels," How We Made It in Africa, January 15, 2018, available at: https://www.howwemadeitinafrica.com/journey-far-bethle-hem-tilahun-alemu-founder-solerebels/60760

[xxxi] Farida Dawkins, "From Africa to the U.S., this Zimbabwean Inventor is Excelling Without Formal Training," Face 2 Face Africa, April 1, 2018, available at: https://face2faceafrica.com/article/from-africa-to-the-u-s-this-zimbabwean-inventor-is-excelling-without-formal-training

[xxxii] Editorial, "Africa's People Must Be Able to Write Their Own Ge-nomics Agenda," Nature, October 28, 2020, available at: https://go.na-ture.com/3XNs62X

xxxiii Emmanuel Aziken,"Iyabo Obasanjo writes father, says: 'Dear Daddy, you don't own Nigeria," Vanguard, December 18, 2013, available at: https://www.vanguardngr.com/2013/12/iyabo-obasanjo-writes-father-says-dear-daddy-dont-nigeria

xxxiv Abdu Rafiu, "Obasanjo and Obasanjo: Letter of an era," The Guardian, January 12, 2023, available at: https://guardian.ng/features/focus/obasanjo-and-obasanjo-letter-of-an-era

xxxv Salieu Taal, "A Hashtag that Inspired Hope," OpenGlobalRights, February 28, 2019, available at: https://www.openglobalrights.org/a-hashtag-that-inspired-hope-gambia-has-decided

xxxvi Seth Onyango, "Africa accounts for 70% of the world's $1 trillion mobile money market," Quartz, May 4, 2022, available at: https://qz.com/africa/2161960/gsma-70-percent-of-the-worlds-1-trillion-mobile-money-market-is-in-africauu

xxxvii Doris Dokua Sasua, "Internet users in Nigeria 2018-2022, with forecasts up until 2027," Statista, December 5, 2022, available at: https://www.statista.com/topics/7199/internet-usage-in-nigeria

xxxviii Simon Kemp, "Digital 2022: Egypt," DataReportal, February 15, 2022, available at: https://datareportal.com/reports/digital-2022-egypt

xxxix Saifaddin Galal, "Social media in Africa – Statistics & Facts," November 17, 2022, available at: https://www.statista.com/topics/9922/social-media-in-africa/#dossierContents__outerWrapper

xl Brayden Lindrea, "Nigeria set to pass bill recognizing Bitcoin and cryptocurrencies," Cointelegraph, December 19, 2022, available at: https://cointelegraph.com/news/nigeria-set-to-pass-bill-recognizing-bitcoin-and-cryptocurrencies

[xli] Chatham House, "What Makes a Successful Protest?," December 15, 2020, available at: https://www.chathamhouse.org/2020/12/what-makes-successful-protest

[xlii] National Geographic, "Africa: Human Geography," Resource Library, Encyclopedic Entry, available at: https://education.nationalgeographic.org/resource/africa-human-geography

[xliii] Becky Bach, "Mind this: Research reveals the power of the mind," Scope, Stanford Medicine, June 18, 2018, available at: https://scopeblog.stanford.edu/2018/06/18/mind-this-research-reveals-the-power-of-the-mind. See also: https://www.linkedin.com/pulse/5-scientific-studies-prove-power-positive-thinking-mark-guidi

[xliv] The Conversation via Yahoo News, "5 Elections to watch in 2023 – what's at stake as millions head to the ballot box around the globe," December 26, 2021, available at: https://news.yahoo.com/5-elections-watch-2023-whats-145510360.html?fr=sycsrp_catchall

[xlv] BBC News, "How has Rwanda saved the lives of 590,000 children?," April 29, 2015, available at: https://www.bbc.com/news/world-africa-32438104